Soccer

Julie Murray

Abdo
SPORTS HOW TO
Kids

abdopublishing.com

Published by Abdo Kids, a division of ABDO, P.O. Box 398166, Minneapolis, Minnesota 55439. Copyright © 2018 by Abdo Consulting Group, Inc. International copyrights reserved in all countries. No part of this book may be reproduced in any form without written permission from the publisher. Abdo Kids Junior™ is a trademark and logo of Abdo Kids.

Printed in the United States of America, North Mankato, Minnesota.

102017

012018

Photo Credits: iStock, Shutterstock, United States Air Force, ©Michael Barera p.22/CC-BY-SA 4.0, ©Johan Elisson p.22/CC-BY-SA 3.0, ©Ronnie Macdonald p.22/CC-BY 2.0

Production Contributors: Teddy Borth, Jennie Forsberg, Grace Hansen

Design Contributors: Christina Doffing, Candice Keimig, Dorothy Toth

Publisher's Cataloging-in-Publication Data

3 1907 00395 4186

Names: Murray, Julie, author.

Title: Soccer / by Julie Murray.

Description: Minneapolis, Minnesota : Abdo Kids, 2018. | Series: Sports how to |
        Includes glossary, index and online resource (page 24).

Identifiers: LCCN 2017943131 | ISBN 9781532104169 (lib.bdg.) | ISBN 9781532105289 (ebook) |
        ISBN 9781532105845 (Read-to-me ebook)

Subjects: LCSH: Soccer--Juvenile literature. | Soccer--History--Juvenile literature.

Classification: DDC 796.334 --dc23

LC record available at https://lccn.loc.gov/2017943131

Table of Contents

Soccer

Sue loves soccer! She is ready to play.

jersey

ball

cleat

shin guard

5

Soccer is played on a field.

Each team has 11 players.

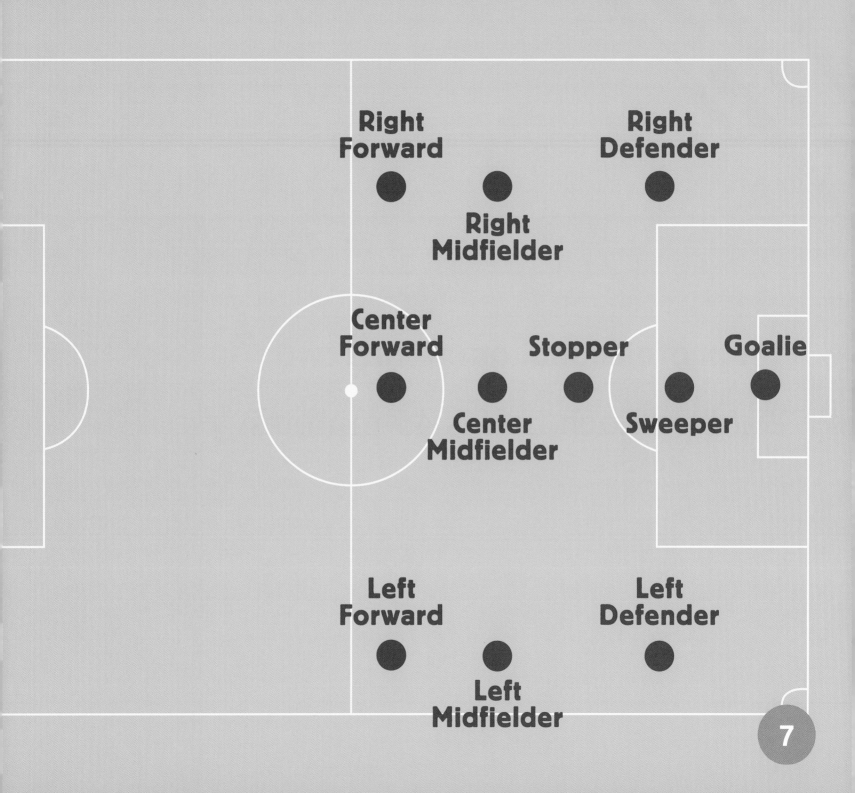

Right Forward

Right Defender

Right Midfielder

Center Forward

Stopper

Goalie

Center Midfielder

Sweeper

Left Forward

Left Defender

Left Midfielder

A **professional** game has two halves. Each half is 45 minutes.

Players cannot use their hands. They use their feet.

Each team tries to put the ball in the net. It is one point.

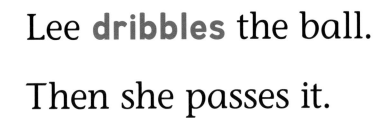

Lee **dribbles** the ball.

Then she passes it.

Alex is close to the net.

She takes a shot.

Evan is the goalie. He stops the ball. Goalies can use their hands.

Ike has a **breakaway**. He kicks the ball into the net. Goal!

Some Ways to Resume Play in Soccer

corner kick

free kick

goal kick

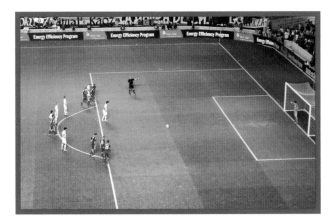

penalty kick

Glossary

breakaway
an offensive play where the player with the ball moves ahead of defenders and toward the goal.

dribble
to move a ball by repeated light kicks.

professional
a sport where players receive payment for their performance.

Index

Abdo Kids
ONLINE
FREE! ONLINE MULTIMEDIA RESOURCES

Visit **abdokids.com** and use this code to access crafts, games, videos, and more!

Abdo Kids Code:
SSK4169